Table of Contents

Introduction

Accomplishing goals and tasks are a worthwhile way of achieving self actualization. They are also a way to find other worthwhile opportunities, but only if you reach those deadlines on time. There are many of us who although, are capable of completing our tasks, might feel compelled to put them off until a later time. The habit of doing that can and should be changed ultimately leading to being more productive and feeling better about ourselves.

The world dictionary recognises this as procrastination. Procrastination as a verb, functions to defer, or delay actions. Not a verb many of want to be associated with, but find ourselves drawn into a chronic cycle of, on a day to day basis. If you're giving up on tasks without taking the time to see them through or running out on a deadline because you were too busy playing solitaire on your computer, you may be a procrastinator who gradually loses interest in accomplishing things because they became distracted.

Are your fears confirmed? And do you feel go into a mode of self lashing and an hour long guilt trip recognising that you have a hard time completing tasks just because you're lacking the will power to continue with the actual tasks?

Fear not! This book is here to help you!

This book will challenge your thought process and work on getting you back on track. Procrastination may seem like a simple practice that can be overcome by ignoring your hang-ups with whatever you need to accomplish, but between those hang-ups and the deadlines there are several things you can do to overcome your habit of procrastination.

Why do we procrastinate – Do you just like to play safe?

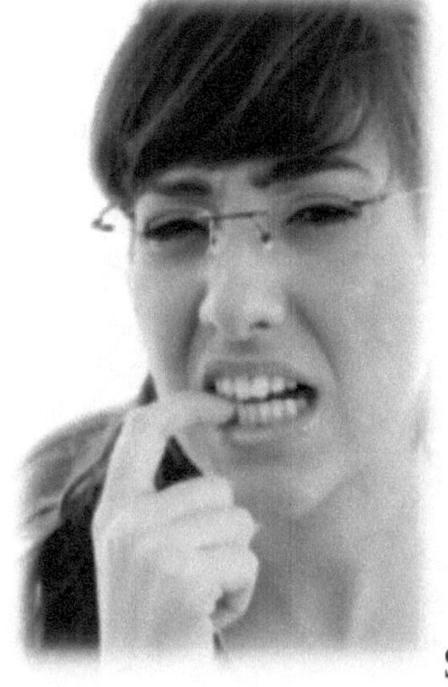

Studies show that 20% of all adults, whether they might be men or women are chronic procrastinators. In order to broach the subject of how to kick the 'habit', you should try to figure out your style of procrastination. This is a small step in figuring out what your strategy to overcome your style of procrastination may be. Procrastination is more to do with a person's nature and general psychology than it is to do with our physical well being. This is why procrastination styles differ from one another because you may get distracted from a task for a different reason then some others.

Procrastination styles

The perfectionist

Are you by nature, a perfectionist? Do you like your ideas laid out in a certain format before you begin your work? Do you have an overpowering need for the heading of an assignment to be in a perfect alignment on your page or you can't continue with writing any further? Then you're a perfectionist who can't start a project of finish it because you're worried the smallest insignificant details may not be perfect.

The dreamer

Do most of your thought processes over a project or task involve floundering ideas, which are vague? Are you imaginative or creative enough to think up of stories and just get stuck executing them because you find that doing any actual work towards completing a project is tedious and boring? Then you're a dreamer. You like to think up or various ideas, but you would rather that some miracle save you from the work that goes into giving those ideas life.

The worrier

Are your thoughts haunted by constant self doubt and doubts over your ability to see through a project, which may be new for you or put you outside of your comfort zone? Do you stumble and abandon a project because mentally you're unable to shut off the constant 'what if's' in your mind? If so, then you are a worrier who finds it hard to start or complete a project because they are doubtful of their own abilities to see a task through.

The defier

Are you one those people who doesn't like to be 'told' to do something? Are you avoiding a responsibility because you feel pressured and oppressed to do it in the first place? Then you are prone to defying authority through your procrastination by not completing a project on a given deadline, or simply not starting a project because you feel defiant in the face of being asked to complete it.

The crises makers

Are you an adrenaline junkie? Does a project have to be exciting to take the edge off for you and make you commit to completing it? Do you feel compelled to leave a project until it's almost due to start because the race to finish it might excite you more? Then you're a crises maker who procrastinates because they need some kind of adrenaline rush, in order to get them physically moving towards starting and finishing a project.

The over-doer

Are you complacent in accepting various projects because you suffer from the inability to say 'no' and later resent the amount of work on your table? Do you find it hard to turn anyone down, and end up over stretched and burnt out, unable to finish anything and start others? Then you're an over-doer who stretches themselves thin and takes on more work than they can actually handle.

Have you managed to identify your style of procrastination from this list? If you have, give yourself some points because you've just accomplished the first step to kicking your habit of procrastination. These styles are the legs your procrastination stands on. Kick these legs out from under your habit by taking another step towards productivity.

The next chapter will talk about more reasons for procrastination

Break the Safety Mould – Identify Your Procrastination Triggers

For those of us who don't fit in the mould of the above procrastination styles, and find ourselves productive for a period of time and then revert back to the habit of letting our priorities slide, don't let yourself fall into a vicious cycle of putting unimportant things before things you know you need to do.

The best way to do this is to identify what triggers your cycle of procrastination. As mentioned earlier on in the book, procrastination has more to do with your perfunctory mental status than it does with anything else. The human brain is a complex organ, yet it can easily get sidetracked by a myriad of things productive people overcome every day.

So, what are your triggers?

Time wastage

This is the simplest and most common trigger that makes us fall back on our deadlines, or ignore or tasks a while longer. What do you waste time on instead of doing starting a project? We all go on the occasional check through of our social media accounts, which have amounted to ridiculous numbers, Face book, Twitter, Snap chat, Whatsapp, Instagram, etc.

Living in an internet aware age, everyone and anyone we know are on those sites and it's not hard to get lost in a myriad of notifications, alerts, photos, videos, and trends out there. You may not realise how much time you're spending on an average, just checking your messages or replying back to comments. While, it is in no way the fault of social media, but you know it's a trigger for you, when you continue checking for updates on your social media accounts instead of carrying on with a task.

This isn't the only way you might find your procrastination cycle triggered; you may put off work a little longer in order to catch up on the latest episode of your favourite show, or may feel the irreverent need to re-watch a series from the start. This trigger may seem harmless; and you may admittedly think it's your tendency to willingly waste your time on these activities that causes a trigger and not the activities themselves, but if you're a procrastinator and you know that you waste time on social media and other electronic media then it may be best to set a time for these things, making sure you don't miss out on finishing an important project.

Time mismanagement

This is similar to the above trigger, but different because some of us may be able to set an appropriate time for social media excursions, but may be unable to visualise the time we may need to get a project finished.

You may agree to a deadline that you're too slow to finish, or you may not be able to keep appointments you make and by committing to a deadline you may find yourself with an issue of mismanagement of time. This can easily upset the healthy balance of productivity and may cause you to seek fulfilment in other activities compared to a task that needs your attention. Learn to manage your time better, by consistently reviewing tasks and keeping appointments you make.

Afraid of failure

The fear of impending failure can be a big trigger and can cause you to lose sight of a deadline and disrupt your priorities. Even though, it seems inconceivable that just the fear of rejection, or dislike of your work by a boss, co-worker can cause you enough anxiety to make you wary of completing a job and realising your own potential.

Success is subjective, some people consider getting a good review of your work to be the ultimate success, but the real measure of success is putting yourself out there and allowing others to judge you. Failure is an important part of life and it is seen as a learning curve towards ultimate success. Don't let fear drive you away from work or miss deadlines, approach your tasks head on and kick your habit of procrastination!

Focus issues

Do you find your attention wavering from task to task without any clear focus because of noise in the background, loud music, social media usage, tiredness, etc? Reduced focus is sometimes self induced and sometimes you're unable to focus on a project because you didn't sleep well.

Even things we eat have an effect on whether we stay focused on a task. Find out why you're unable to focus on your task. Is it something simple like electronic media distractions? Which, you could easily detract from by limiting your use of them when you're trying to finish a task.

Eat foods that don't weigh you down, and make you sleepy. The more focused you are, the better are your chances of kicking the habit of procrastination.

Dislike for the task you need to do

This can be another driving factor, which controls your trigger mechanism for your procrastination habit. If you find the task ahead unpleasant, or don't like what you do, you may be tempted to look for other forms of self fulfilment.

The task that needs your attention may slip from your priorities easily because you feel it's not beneficial to your success, or development. For example, if you hate washing dishes and a pile of dishes is laying in the sink waiting for you as you walk into the kitchen the next morning, you might find yourself flitting from task to task, avoiding the dishes until you realise that you don't have any clean dishes for dinner.

The easy thing would really be to just wash them and get it over with instead of lingering on other irrelevant tasks that could wait. Make the dishes your priority and don't allow them to hang over your head as something you 'still' need to do.

Indecisiveness

Indecision can be a big cause of stress for some chronic procrastinators and hinder your progress in a project. You may be unable to decide what angle to take on an article, you might be unsure of what colour to paint your room despite the varying shades of white at hand, etc.

All the, what if's, and maybe-I-should-think-about-it-over-a-movie-or-coffee-break are just your average time stealers and procrastination encouragers. Pick a colour and stick to it, don't let indecision waste your time and tire you out before you can even start on a project.

Indecisiveness isn't just a time waster; it's also an energy drainer. Going wild over minute details that won't matter later on are sure fire ways of mentally exhausting yourself out of completing a task you set out to accomplish.

Taking more than you can chew off

It's easy to get carried away when you're doing better and your procrastination is down to a minimum level. Taking on more than you can actually accomplish might get you right back into that unyielding zone of procrastination that stretches on whenever you feel exhaustion pricking at you.

Learn to know and understand your strengths. How much is too much for you? Don't take on more projects than you can handle at a given time, otherwise you're going to end up burnt out and stressed to even think about starting another task. Give yourself some well timed breaks, not going overboard and just focusing on relaxation.

Coach your brain back to productivity!

Unrelated stress or pressure

Are you suffering from some underlying stress of life that has nothing to do with the tasks you're meant to accomplish? And you do you find yourself hard pressed to start on a project? Daily life stresses are common and unavoidable because of everyday life complexities. If you don't cope well with them, you may end up on the procrastination cycle more often than you think.

Learning to cope with daily life pressures and stresses is an important step in getting back on track with your tasks. It helps you to remain focused. If you're too busy thinking about some fallout you had with a friend, you may end up losing precious time thinking of all the things you could have said to stop things from going awry.

Separate your priorities from your issues and you will find that it's easier to come back from the brink of a never ending procrastination cycle. Find out what combination of reasons causes you to procrastinate so, that you can make your own strategy to combat these issues and become productive again.

Strategies to Overcome Procrastination

A combination of above reasons could be your issue for falling into the habit. Most of us don't realise that sheer willpower or deadlines aren't enough for chronic procrastinators to get back to good productivity levels. Now that we've talked about varying reasons for our procrastination over projects, let's take a look at some strategies, which will bring back your confidence and help you fight the habit! Approach these strategies with positive thoughts and find yourself in a better place then you were before you began reading the book.

1. Establish S.M.A.R.T. goals

Goals are like road maps. If you're trying to start a task you need to establish guidelines to achieving this task. Turn your looming/unfinished tasks into clear, achievable goals.

A general example of setting a goal would go something like this: your boss expects a certain report on his desk, in no more than two days from now.

In setting your goal you should be able to plan how to get this report done. Example,

- How soon before handing over the report do you have to review it?
- How quickly can you finish it before reviewing it for any errors and problems?
- How much of the report will you actually be able to complete each day until it's time to submit it?

Answering all these questions honestly and with clarity will give you a general idea on how to handle a task when it comes to you, but setting S.M.A.R.T goals are an even better way to get better results while setting goals.

S.M.A.R.T stands for specific, measurable, attainable, realistic, and timely goals. If your goals can encompass these qualities, you're on your way to your tasks being accomplished with more efficiency.

Specific goals: A general goal will be that you want to get in shape, but a more specific goal will help you choose a direction to tackle this task. A better goal would be to that you're looking to lose a certain amount of weight, in a designated amount of time, by working out in the gym for x number of days a week.

See the difference between the general goal and a specific one? It makes a huge difference when you know exactly what you want to achieve. This way you can make the required changes in your life to achieve it.

In order to set a specific goal you may want to start by answering the 6 W's

Who: Are you the only one involved in achieving this goal? Is someone else required to help?

When: Identify a timeline for achieving the goal.

Where: Where can you achieve this goal? Is the location important?

Why: What are the benefits to you of achieving this goal?

Which: Identify obstacles and requirement for the goal.

What: What do you want to accomplish exactly?

Once you answer these questions you can get to work with a clearer objective, time frame, and ability to achieve the goal.

Measurable goals: Turn your long winded task into measurable goals. It's important to use time constraints to measure you progress during a task. Manage your goals by measuring the time it will take to finish certain parts, or the entire task.

Ask yourself questions like:

How long will it take me to complete an x number of pages?
How many pages do I need to complete in order to finish the task?

This will help you set goals that coincide with deadlines.

Attainable goals: Setting goals that are attainable will give you a feeling of great achievement when you attain them, but it's easier if you set goals that have a realistic sense to them. Imagine your doctor tells you to get in shape, and you decide to do this by changing your diet and exercising for an hour every day. You may find yourself unable to exercise for an hour everyday if you've never exercised before and may need to build the stamina for it over time. Also, resorting to eating lower calories then you're used to may also prove difficult if you've never done this before.

Once you find out your goal is not really attainable, you may feel overwhelmed and negativity can set in easily, eating away at your desire to get into shape. Viola! You start to procrastinate and just put the exercising away for another day in the future. Set goals that are simpler to achieve with your present capabilities, and you are less likely to procrastinate because you will be on your way to accomplishing your goal.

Realistic goals: Think about what makes any goal achievable? The ability to complete a task greatly depends on the fact that it's a goal, which is realistically achievable. When you set out to make goals, make sure that you're aiming only as high as you can reach. You need to be able to work towards finishing the goal itself.

The saying, 'where there's a will, there is a way' goes a long way in helping achieve even the most difficult goals, but if you're goal is unrealistic, like a project due in an unrealistic time frame, or deadline, you're not likely to succeed. A 100 page report is next to impossible to complete in 3-4 hours, so don't set yourself up for failure before you even begin. Setting realistic goals makes you more likely to succeed and find ways to complete a task much more easily because you're not hindered by the stress of not being able to achieve the goals you set for yourself.

Timely goals: No goal is complete without a real timeframe in which to expedite, complete, or attain the goal. If you decide to lose weight and don't set a tentative time limit like x number of pounds in x number of weeks, you're likely fall back into the habit of procrastination. There will be no real urgency to actually do anything to achieve the goal you self for yourself.

Grounding yourself to a timeframe is a way of committing to your goal and making sure the outcome positively benefits you, otherwise a goal without a time limit is likely to become a task which will drag on and on until you seal it with a deadline for yourself. Self deadlines are more important than the deadlines set for you by a boss, or a teacher.

Setting an appropriate deadline helps you in completing your work on time, giving you plenty of opportunity to review it, correct mistakes, or any other issues, and also helps discipline those of us who are prone to procrastination.

2. Visualise your goals

Visualization has always been referred to as a powerful tool, which can help in the accomplishment of goals, but here we will use visualisation to help motivate us, make us more focused, and activate us to complete our tasks.

Break the chains of procrastination by being productive, and the best way to complete any task and reach goals you set for yourself is to visualise your motivation to achieve them. With enough motivation you are unlikely to continue with your routine procrastination. So, how does one go about visualizing their motivation?

It's a process you can learn over time:

1. Find a quiet, peaceful place where you feel you will not be disturbed.

2. Once you've found a quiet spot, close your eyes and think about the mood, skill, behaviour, and goal you want to acquire.

3. Now relax yourself and take several deep breaths.

4. Start by visualizing the situation you desire in your head as clearly and in as much detail as you can.

5. To this vision, add feelings and emotions you wish to achieve once accomplish your goal.

6. Practice visualising in this manner two times a day for at least 10 minutes each time.

7. Keep at this until you feel you've achieved enough positive motivation to go on and start, or carry on with your task, while maintaining these positive thoughts.

Use visualization as a technique to achieve your goals and end the constant cycle of procrastination some of us suffer from. Positive imagery will not only motivate you, but will also help you acquire new positive behaviours, emotions, and improves your focus.

3. Break your goals into smaller activities

Even measurable goals can be harder to achieve if you don't break your
goals into smaller activities, which can be much easier to achieve than
attempting the entire task at one time. You can't finish fifty pages of
writing a report in 2 days without dividing the number of pages by the
time you have until the deadline.

If a task seems too big to complete, break it down into small tasks,
making your job smaller. This will ease your mind about the projects
size and your deadline to finish the entire job won't seem like its staring
you down the entire time. Shrinking a task helps you focus better on
quality and motivates you to move on to the next one quicker. You won't
feel procrastination kicking in this way and you can manage your time
better when you continually finish the mini tasks leading up to the
accomplishment of a goal. This way, you won't feel like you can't finish
a task because of the sheer size of it.

4. Build bridges of accountability

Being accountable for a task means being responsible for the completion of a job you previously procrastinated on. If you do it right, accountability won't feel like a liability instead of another step into becoming more productive. Accountability helps motivate you to complete tasks before deadlines can hit you. Make a to-do list each day and put your goals or tasks on them. After the day is over, check the things you've done and circle the ones that still remain.

This is the first step in being accountable to yourself. When you make a to-do list, you acknowledge that you have a task to complete and that once that task is completed you can check it off your list, thereby equating a successful day. If you were unable to complete a task, list the reasons for this. The easiest thing to do next would be to break your task into smaller jobs and put them on the to-do list again the next day and then try to get them done.

This is one way of being accountable; another is to be accountable to someone else instead of you. You can do this by telling someone; a friend, a spouse, etc. what you are planning to do that day and have them check in on you, or ask you whether you completed the task. If you're a procrastinator, this will be a good way to build accountability and make you eager to finish a task so that you feel positive about yourself and your ability to accomplish any project.

5. Reward your accountability

This is an easy, if not an enjoyable strategy to have, if your method of gaining accountability is successful, you should reward yourself, to strengthen positive behaviour in yourself, and to encourage the avoidance of negative consequences of not completing a task on time through procrastination.

Now, rewarding your positive step to productivity doesn't have to be expensive, it can be something small, like extra time on social media. If social media was a distraction for you earlier, you will learn to enjoy it in a more controlled manner through rewarding yourself for not being lazy on a task.

6. Get a handle on your fears

We talked about having a general fear of failure, and some of us having a penchant for perfectionism, which makes us give up even before we began a task. What can you do about this? Be brave!

Embrace your fears without the stress of worrying about small details and nitpicking on things that are not really that important in the long run.

Just start a task and think about corrections and errors midway, and make yourself content with the idea that you can't control every small detail about the task. The best way to get a handle on most of these fears, including ones that involve self doubt over your own capabilities, is to give yourself positive affirmations.

Affirmations are positive statements, which can change your negative emotions and thoughts to positive ones. By believing these affirmations your entire attitude to a task can change.

Try some of these statements for your affirmations:

- I will stick to my deadline.
- I am fully capable of finishing this task.
- I am talented and creative.
- I'm going to stick to the plans I make.
- Small errors don't bother me.

- I'm going to start my project and stay motivated to finish it.

These simple statements are nothing but words on their own, but they can be used as powerful tools of motivation, if you train your brain to believe them.

How can you do this? This is as simple as visualizing your goals:

a. The first step is to think of all your positive attributes and write them down on a piece of paper. This will help you to get rid of negative sentiments of self doubt you encounter while trying to complete a task. Start every sentence with an 'I', example;

I am intelligent and bright.
OR
I am full of great ideas.

b. Now think of the goals you want to accomplish, or the tasks you want to complete. This is like a check list, only you will use the positive affirmations to motivate your mind towards completing them. Be specific with your goals. Also make a list of the negative sentiments you have about your own capabilities or negative traits you want to change about yourself.

Goals:
I need to finish 10 pages of writing before I sleep.
OR
I need to empty the trash every day before going off to bed.

Negative traits:
I overeat at night.
I ignore my to-do list.
I keep putting off my work for later.

c. Now you can start on writing your positive affirmations, starting them all with 'I can' OR 'I will'. This is to affirm to yourself that you can do a particular task. Example;

I can finish my reading.
OR
I will finish my work by the given deadline.

Try keeping these statements as short, clear, and positive as
possible.

d. The next step is to match some of your positive attributes with
    the goal oriented affirmations you wrote down for yourself. For
    example; if you need to finish a project on time, match your
    positive attribute of being creative and full of ideas with your
    goal of finishing 10 pages before you sleep. Match two or three
    of your positive attributes to this goal.

e. Make a point of writing down all your affirmations and
    repeating them to yourself, over and over. This is the best way
    to make them effective as an approach to change a negative
    mind set, or remedy lethargic behaviour. Make sure your
    affirmations are the first thing you think of when you get up in
    the morning and the last thing you think of before going to
    sleep.

f. From time to time in the day sit in a quiet place and meditate
    over these affirmations. Repeating them to yourself until you're
    sure something in your mind has relented and accepted them as
    true. Think about emotion these statements evoke in you and let
    them bring about a positive change in your mind and body.

g.   Put your affirmations on post it's and stick them to refrigerator door as reminders. Think about what the words means to you every time you pass them by. Carry your affirmations with you in your purse or wallet and read them if you feel yourself wavering from your goals.

h. When you accomplish some goal, reaffirm your positive statements to yourself and continue using them to be further productive.

7. Daily, weekly, monthly reviews of tasks or goals

Review of tasks, completed and leftover can be a very helpful tool in combating of procrastination. Make yourself accountable to this review and become more motivated to complete tasks on time. You can do this in several different ways, you can make a daily review chart of your achievements and any task which were left uncompleted, or you could opt for weekly reviews of your performance to see how much you've managed to accomplish a week's time.

Small tasks can be reviewed daily and will keep the pressure off of you for achieving larger goals. The larger tasks can be scheduled for a weekly review to see the amount of your progress and how quickly you're making it to the finish line.

Review long term plans and goals with a monthly review of overall work you've done. This way you can keep track of what you're doing and how much you're doing. This is also a great way to monitor your levels of procrastination and what you're doing to avoid this. The idea that you may be accountable to your own checklist can spur you to work more and be even more productive.

You can use all these strategies, or even some of them in combination, to help turn around your habit of procrastination. It can be addictive to just stop being productive once you're in a chronic cycle of procrastination, but these strategies will definitely pick you up and bring out your productive side.

Make an Important Things Checklist (ITC) to overcome procrastination

The eighth strategy to overcome procrastination is to make a checklist and use it. Consider pilots on an airplane; they have several checklists that they need to go through before they can even take off. Unless they make sure every item on their check list is handled, they can encounter difficulties during a flight.

By now you must have gotten the idea that checklists are an important part your journey to get rid of procrastination. Checklists may appear as a formality you'd rather forego in favour of just starting your day, but these checklists are there to remind you of tasks you need to complete. They remind you of what you've not finished, and they even hold you somewhat accountable to yourself.

Making a list of tasks makes you more likely to avoid the need to start on a procrastination cycle. The human memory isn't infallible; you may forget some of the things you needed to do because of the vast number of things you need to finish in a day.

- Just make a checklist to keep yourself informed and ready to finish a task and check them off each time you finish something. This can be done by making three types of checklists.

- Make a checklist of the areas you're prone to procrastinate in.

- Make a checklist on your productivity to counter procrastination.

- Make a checklist of the actual tasks, or goals you need to accomplish.

The first checklist will tell you the areas you tend to procrastinate in, and will help you figure out a pattern. It will tell you whether you're levels of procrastination are high or low, and should also give you an idea of what activities to avoid in order to reduce the amount of procrastination to resort to.

Let's look at an example of what this checklist should look like. You can add subtract things to it as you like, depending on what tasks you're worried about procrastinating on:

Checklist 1: Where do I procrastinate?

Health and wellbeing

- Sleep well/ Get at least 7 hours of sleep? ___
- Get some exercise ___
- Eat well today ___

Work

- Get to work on time ___
- Use my break wisely___
- Calls to return/make ___
- Communicate with the boss ___
- Interaction with colleague's ___

Home

- Cooking ___
- Cleaning ___
- Washing ___
- Errands ___
- Pay bills ___
- Family commitments ___

Relationships

- Make time for friend's ___
- Meet new people ___
- Make time for family ___
- Remember special occasions ___
- Other ___

Other

- Long term goals
- Home maintenance
- Car repairs

- Income taxes

Checklist 2: Where can I improve productivity?

The second checklist will help you to realise how to go about attempting to start on a task because this checklist is all about productivity and the things that can increase your levels of productivity.

Let's look at an example of what this checklist should look like, you can add subtract things to it as you like:

Tasks you need to complete/get started on? _____

Broken tasks into smaller jobs ____

All distractions are off (Social media, electronic devices, etc.) _____

You're well hydrated _____

Inspirational quotes on walls/music to inspire you is on _____

Take a break every forty five minutes ______

Finished your work _____

Checklist 3: Tasks and Deadlines to be met

The third one is simple, you write down your tasks along with their deadlines if necessary. It depends on the size of the task and how much time you have to complete it. If you've broken down tasks into smaller jobs, even better! As and when you finish the jobs on this checklist, you can tick them off.

Write down what the task is? ___

What parts did you break down the task into? List them ___

A Introduction + chapter 1+ chapter 2

B Chapter 3 + chapter 4

C Conclusion + references

Write down what rewards you will feel/receive when you finish the work ___

Ways in which you could make the task fun (have fun with it) ____

Chart your time for each task against time constraints you've set for yourself ___

Tips for making any of your checklists

Tackling tasks can be easier if you have a written plan for yourself, but if you feel a   bit lost when you start on making your own checklists, you can count on these tips to make efficient checklists, which not only get you motivated, but also cover every detail of your task until you finish them successfully:

- Make simple and clear checklists, which are straightforward.

- Always start with the things that are most important and need to be done immediately so that you will feel productive after they are done.

- Pace yourself. Balance the time setting on the tasks in your checklist, whichever one it may be, so that you're not multitasking and getting yourself overwhelmed.

- Avoid over planning to make plan perfect, this will only make you procrastinate further. Checklists should be easy and simplified so that you don't feel daunted starting on your tasks.

- Spend a few minutes reviewing your progress. DON'T forget to review! Otherwise you may forget something that needed doing, or may lose momentum if you spend too much time looking at the checklist. Just review it and move on to the next item.

- The tasks on your checklists should match your goals and values, otherwise you won't feel energetic enough to start them or finish them.

- Break each step of a task into different steps on your task checklist so that when you finish each step you gain more confidence and momentum.

- Spread any large tasks over several work sessions and set completion points for every task so that you have something to looks forward to when you pass them.

Tips To Remain Productive and Avoid Procrastination

You've almost made it, you're starting over, and you are going to start getting some work finished! When you start to take steps towards fighting the urge to procrastinate, you are automatically making some progress, but don't derail this progress with minor mistakes that may put all your initial hard work to waste. No one is perfect there will always be chances to procrastinate and waste time. One might say, the opportunities to not do the work are virtually endless, but there are several tips and tricks you can use to counter these negative feeling and move ahead of them in spite of whatever tends to hold you back generally.

Draw on these tips to keep yourself going in a positive direction:

1. Just start! Do it! Don't go the perfectionist route and wait for things to be perfect or you will lose focus and pass your deadline. Tasks get done, when you make a move to start on them, not by waiting for the right time.

2. Decide on how much you can get done at a time, don't overwhelm yourself with too much at a time. This is another way of overexerting yourself and giving up on your work.

3. Aim for progress rather that perfectionism.

4. Do the most difficult job first and get it out of the way.

5. Alternate these difficult jobs with jobs you like to make it enjoyable.

6. Notice all your interruptions and what they are caused by, so that you can avoid them the next time you're working on a task.

7. Delegate things you can't do yourself and don't be afraid to ask for help.

8. Make sure you have a good, comfortable place to work and the best tools for working.

9. Make sure your desk is clean and organised before you start working, so that you aren't visually distracted.

10. Stop thinking of the task as a chore and think of it as the progress you're making.

11. Stay motivated by keeping yourself accountable to someone, a friend, spouse, partner, etc.

12. Reward yourself on your accomplishments, even a small bag of M&M to celebrate your progress is a great way to keep yourself motivated yourself.

13. Whenever you feel like pausing and are starting to procrastinate, think of everything you will feel like when

you've finished a particular task.

14. Get some exercise and fresh air, this will clear your head and pump you up for more work.

15. Eat healthy things that encourage a good mental state and boosts brain activity. Things like green vegetables, nuts, and omega 3 supplements are great for boosting your brain activity and make you feel healthier.

16. The bigger your accomplishment, the bigger reward you should give yourself.

17. To avoid getting distracted by social media notifications, etc. you should log out of your accounts on the computer, I pad, or phone, you use. And then log back in after you complete your tasks. If you aren't logged in you won't immediately think of pausing while working.

18. Check your emails a minimum of twice daily.

19. Create a routine for yourself because it is an effective way of keeping yourself focused and motivated.

20. Prioritize your work; get to the critical work first.

21. Find a way to get the boring/tough stuff done in a different manner then general. If you have large spreadsheets to work on in excel, find a way to automate it, to get it done easier.

22. Surround yourself with motivated people, whose positivity will rub off on you.

23. Pay attention to your energy at day time and night time. Find out whether you're more productive at night, or at day, get more stuff done whenever you're more energetic.

24. Don't worry about failure, you can always start from the beginning again. The biggest worry for those of us who procrastinate is that we may fall back into the habit. Even if that does happen you can always re-strategize and get yourself back on track.

25. Study the strong points and motivational habits of others. This is a good way of finding out how you can improve on your system and do things better.

26. Do what you enjoy, and you will never suffer from procrastination again! Invest in some soul searching and find what you're passionate about.

27. Use these tips in conjunction with your strategies to meet procrastination head on.

28. Start writing a motivational journal and note down things you do differently that motivated you to do better. It doesn't have to be complex, just simply keep track of your motivational triggers as you would keep track of your procrastination triggers.

29. Tell yourself today is a good day to get started on your tasks, not tomorrow.

Myths about Procrastination

Commonly, many of us resort to procrastination because we can't be asked to do the work ahead of us and make common excuses to cope with our lack of productivity, as a way of rationalising what we know is wrong. So, if you resort to any of these myths while working, beware!

'Procrastination isn't harmful to me otherwise. I'll just pull a few all nighters to complete the job'

Sounds easy doesn't it? Giving into procrastinating with the firm belief that you'll finish working when you're mentally recharged, but this is only a coping mechanism. What if you're too exhausted physically and mentally to actually work at night? You pretty much end up losing that little bit of time as well as the time you promised yourself to get anything done. More like a lose-lose situation.

Not only will you be too tired to work on the important stuff, pulling on all nighters to get your work done maybe harmful to your health. If you don't sleep well, you won't feel recharged enough the next day to be any more productive than you were yesterday.

'It only has to do with managing time'

Procrastination is the product of many things, from intentional ignoring of a task to spending your day doing other meaningless things. Time management is an important concept, but it's not the only thing that you're doing wrong. Furthermore, procrastinators view time differently from generally productive variety of people. For procrastinators, time is a detail that isn't important enough to panic about a deadline because they base their schedule on their other activities first.

'I'll just check my email, social media app for 2 minutes'

Your intentions might be completely noble, but once you pass that 5 minute mark, and get to answering emails, which could wait, or get involved in chatting with an old friend you haven't talked into a while, instead of finishing your work, you're effectively going to end up spend at least 45 minutes on your email or Facebook page and by the time you realise you're meant to get back to work, about ten other things online have distracted you;

an invite from a friend to an event, some online thread that can wait to be read by you . So, your two minutes will end up being 2 hours instead of 2 minutes.

'I'll do it tomorrow because I'll be more motivated tomorrow.'

Motivating yourself to get a task is a great way to beat procrastination. What doesn't work is waiting for a particular brand of motivation to hit you, before you can get to the task. That kind of motivation level might never hit you when you expect it to. You'll just end up wasting weeks over it. Motivation is the product of mental coaching and physical productivity. You can't achieve it, unless you stop procrastinating and actually make the effort to motivate yourself for a task.

'I work much better under pressure'

Working under pressure can produce great results for some of us, but this is subjective, if you're mental capacity is better under pressure, it doesn't automatically imply that you'll be physically adept at handling the pressure to complete the task at the heels of a deadline. Physically you may be too tired to finish on time, or you may be too busy panicking to do a good job on the task. Working under pressure is great, if it doesn't involve you compromising on time and quality of a project. Beyond that it's just an excuse to keep on procrastinating.

'Procrastination doesn't have to be a bad thing; I'll just get other things out of the way before completing my work'

So, you'll take care of an important task what's wrong with that? In the mean time you can get other irrelevant work out of the way. So, that it doesn't bother you when you're starting on an important task. Sadly, procrastination is still defined as putting off your work for another day. It's no better to get those other minor things out of the way, while the important job still sits on your desk waiting for some initiative from you. You're only giving into procrastination and depending on coping tasks to get by without having to do your work.

'I need x number of uninterrupted hours to do the job'

It's great to want to work interrupted and finish the job once and for all. Except, it's not realistic to work uninterrupted for a length of time without hydrating yourself, going to the bathroom, taking a short break. It's an unrealistic approach to work you're already late getting finished. What if you're interrupted by someone else, or have kids at home, if you wait for them not to interrupt you while you're working, it may prove difficult to actually start a task and see it through. Don't wait not to be interrupted, just get on with it and the resist the urge to think you'll do it tomorrow, when there are no such interruptions.

Conclusion

In conclusion, procrastination is a bad habit that affects the healthiest and most creative of us. It's slows down our progress and affects our success by making us less productive then our real potential. Working out why you're procrastination is a big step forward to figuring out a solution. Once you've read this book, you'll have sufficient knowledge about your procrastination habits and various strategies to combat these habits effectively.

Don't worry about failure, learn to embrace it as a part of life that teaches us important lessons we can look back on. If you fall back on procrastinating, you can always avoid the triggers and habits, which lead you to procrastinating again. Keep your to-do lists and checklists up-to-date and rely on them for some semblance of control and direction when you feel yourself faltering. Planning is also an important part of your anti procrastination strategy because if you fail to plan, you plan to fail.

To have a good chance of beating procrastination, you need to first identify that you're doing it. Once you've established your issues and know your strategy, be positive and just go for it!

Good luck!